The Day We Finally Came Back from Vietnam

"JUNE 13, 1986"

The Untold Story of Chicago's
WELCOME HOME Veterans Parade

ROGER A MCGILL AND HAROLD F. BEYNE III

"VITA VENTURI SEECULI"

(The life of the world to come)

Print ISBN: 978-1-66789-159-0

Printed in the United States of America on SFI Certified paper.

First Edition

DEDICATION

Tom Stack, Center (photo source: Daily Herald)

This book is dedicated to Tom Stack (09/04/1943 - 04/16/1994) parade innovator, organizer and leader with the deepest gratitude and appreciation for his tireless efforts to pay tribute to the courage and sacrifices of the thousands of men and women who served in Vietnam.

Tom, a platoon leader, served with the U.S. Army, 9th Infantry Division in Vietnam in 1968 – 1969. For his service, he was awarded two Silver Stars, three Bronze Stars for valor, and a number of other awards.

After Vietnam, Tom married Nedra Johnson. They lived a comfortable life in the Mount Greenwood neighborhood on the South side of Chicago with their three children Kristine (Green), Kathryn (Lyons), and Bill.

Tom's career trajectory began as a Chicago policeman. He then taught criminal justice at Daley College. From there, Tom worked with veterans organizations for 15 years. He was a member of the Windy City Vets, VFW Post 5220, American Legion Post 854, Vietnam Veterans of America 207, and later 153, all located on the South side of Chicago.

In May 1985, Tom attended the New York Vietnam Veterans WELCOME HOME Parade, marching in their parade from Battery Park, across the Brooklyn Bridge, down the Cannon of Hero's in a section of Brooklyn. When he came back to Chicago, his aim was clear: he wanted a Chicago Vietnam Veterans WELCOME HOME Parade; his goal was to surpass the 25,000 Vietnam Veterans in the NYC Parade. He did that and more.

Tom was the Chairman of the Chicago Vietnam Veterans Parade Committee, Executive Director of the POW/MIA Run for Freedom, Cook County South Coordinator and Design Selection member of the Illinois Vietnam Veterans Memorial Fund. He went on to be one of the National spokespersons on the Agent Orange issues. Agent Orange was the cause of his cancer and death in 1994.

Tom, along with other Vietnam Veterans, called on then Mayor of Chicago Harold Washington. They requested permission for a parade. The result was the WELCOME HOME parade which is chronicled in this book.

We thank you Tom for allowing all of us to "finally come home from Vietnam".

CONTENTS

PREFACE

"10 Years Late", was the headline covering the 1985 parade in New York City. But as these authors and Tom Stack saw it, this parade really was the preface for the main event: the Chicago WELCOME HOME Vietnam Veterans parade on Friday, June 13, 1986. From a parade of 25,000 veterans in New York, this parade grew to a massive Chicago marching crowd of Vietnam Veterans with estimates ranging from 176,000 to more than 200,000.

The inspiration for this was born in New York City. The innovation however was the brainchild of Tom Stack; the execution was the combined effort of so many other leaders and volunteers ranging from book co-author and parade leader and organizer Roger Mc Gill to volunteer and co-author Harry Beyne to countless other volunteers. Every effort was made to name so many of these individuals, yet it was not possible to name 176,000 veterans who had among their ranks so many who contributed. To those not named, you are not forgotten This event could not have happened without you.

For Vietnam Veterans, this 1986 parade was their homecoming. Or as Roger Mc Gill said after attending the NYC parade "only with this parade did I truly feel that I had finally returned from Vietnam." Hence the title of this book as his statement was uniformly shared by so many who didn't have the opportunity to come to New York but showed up in force for Chicago.

Anyone who has known, loved, honored a Vietnam Veteran understands the pain experienced with their return from war. They were degraded, spat upon, sworn at, and physically abused. Many destroyed their uniforms in shame; others left the country; most refused to talk about the war, their experiences, and their feelings. As a result, so many suffered from physical harm, most suffered from the effects of Agent Orange, and, of course, the silent killer PTSD. Even today, with the average Vietnam Veteran in his or her seventies, many are just now beginning to open up and share with one another. This is a tribute to the efforts of other veterans, their groups, and associations and to many of the dedicated professionals at the Veterans Administration. And there are many. And, yes, there is still a great deal of work to be done. There are veterans who are refusing to get treatment for diseases caused by Agent Orange – if they do, and they are improving or in remission – there is some bean counter who will decide they no longer need disability. This is an uphill battle. But Veterans are heading up the hill.

However, in 1986, they were still at the bottom of the hill. This was just their beginning. This was their Veteran's parade. This was their homecoming. They planned and orchestrated and threw their own party. The good news: the guests poured in. By most counts, more than 500,000 came to celebrate their return, their contributions and to share their appreciation for a job well done.

We extend a heartfelt thank you to all of those who gave so much and to all of those who planned and contributed to this event.

Authors Roger McGill and Harry Beyne in their Vietnam Days

CHAPTER ONE

In the Beginning – from New York to Chicago

As Chicagoans, we really hate to be the second city in terms of welcoming home the Vietnam veterans, 10 years after the fact. But we were second ONLY in terms of having the second parade but in no other terms.

New York's Parade kicked off May 5, 1985. As reported by United Press International (UPI), May 7, 1985, "Mayor Edward I. Koch established the Vietnam Veterans Memorial Commission that organized the parade. He led the march by pushing the wheelchair of John Beehon, a Medal of Honor winner who lost both legs in Vietnam in 1966. Also at the head of the march was Gen. William Westmoreland, who was commander of American forces in Vietnam.... Nineteen Medal of Honor winners participated in the parade, which had the largest number of marchers ever to take part in a Manhattan parade....

It was reported: "There were tens of thousands of Vietnam War veterans who formed the biggest parade in New York City's history, marching across the Brooklyn Bridge and down Broadway in a lavish tickertape "welcome home" with tons of ticker tape and confetti, obliterating street signs in a blizzard of white, showered down on the 25,000 veterans as they wound through the financial district at the lower tip of Manhattan....

"Most of the veterans were dressed in remnants of their uniforms--many of them in jungle fatigues, and many wearing ribbons and medals. Some assembled with their former units, and there were cries of recognition and embraces, and exchanges of photographs and old jokes."

New York City's parade was the start of something that was 10 years late but really needed to happen. More than 25,000 veterans marched.

By the time of the Chicago parade, this number of Veteran marchers was over 176,000.

Chicago and the 25th Infantry Division was well represented.

Chicago Vietnam veterans were there in force, including Parade Organizer and Innovator Tom Stack and book author Roger A. McGill. "We lined up in a Brooklyn Park," explains Roger. "We then marched across the Brooklyn Bridge, down through the City's Canyon of Heroes in New York City listening to the thousands of New Yorkers cheering us on and having the opportunity to be interviewed by a CBS 2 Reporter in that Park when he found out I was from Chicago and why I had come to New York City for this Parade.

"I was staying at the Penta Hotel when I discovered that the 25th Infantry Division had a hospitality Room in the Hotel as well as an Association. I never knew there was an Association; I became a life member and I reconnected with soldiers I met in April in Washington, D.C. when I went to the wall by myself. They told me of the NYC parade and said, "if you go Rog, we will meet you there!" They did. It was the start of life-long friendships."

Those are the pictures also of those of us that served in the 25th Infantry Division in Vietnam at Cu Chi, and we all marched together.

"Some in these pictures are still my friends to this day, and they are from all over the country."

CHAPTER TWO

Bringing it Home: Vietnam Veteran Led and Organized WECOME HOME Parade Launch

"I'll never forget the immediate return to Travis Air Force Base as long as I live," recalled Tom Stack, a platoon leader in 1968 and chairman of the Chicago Vietnam Veterans Parade Committee. "It was horrible. People were pelting servicemen with fruits and tomatoes. Calling them names, scorning them. It was tough to take."

But it was Stack, a criminal justice teacher at Richard J. Daley Community College and holder of two Silver Stars and three Bronze Stars, who made his own dream come true by volunteering about 90 hours of work each week to organize the parade. The idea came to him about a year ago while returning to Chicago from New York, where he had marched alongside 25,000 other veterans.

"Veterans came up to me after the parade and said it made them feel great for the first time in their life to be recognized for what they had done," he said. "For some, all they remember is being called a baby killer or a dope addict when they returned to the States, and they've never talked about Vietnam since then."
(Associated Press, James Litke, June 7, 1986)

"For more than a year, Stack and a group of fellow veterans had sweated, cajoled, begged and borrowed the Chicago parade into existence. The idea of seeing the day when he and his fellow veterans could look back with pride on their service and their sacrifice may have had a special urgency for Stack. He is battling lymph cancer, now in remission after a year and a half of chemotherapy. It is the type of cancer that many thousands of Vietnam veterans now are battling, linked to Agent Orange, the chemical defoliant widely used to uncover

6

the jungle sanctuaries of the enemy." (Authors' note: Tom Stack passed away from this cancer April 16, 1994.)

(Chicago Tribune Magazine, "At Peace at Last: After 11 Years and an Emotional Parade, Vietnam Vets Finally Feel Welcome" William Mullen, 8/17/86).

PARADE ORGANIZERS

Roger, Tom, and a number of others including Julio Gonzales, Larry Langowski, Angelo Terrell, Ken Plummer, Philip Meyer, Connie Edwards, William Davis representing the Mayor's Office came before Alderman Bernie Stone, a member of the City Council of Chicago, who was charged with giving permission to allow for the parade in downtown Chicago. "Our purpose was to present our ideas; to let him know the character and composition of Vietnam Veterans all with the intent of being allowed to organize a Chicago Vietnam Veterans WELCOME HOME Parade," said Roger.

The Alderman gave generously of his time and listened as individually and collectively, group members spoke of the essential need for this parade and their respective and collective views that this parade must be all inclusive – representing all races, genders, and areas of Chicago – enfolding all our Veterans who served this country in Vietnam.

Alderman Stone assembled the information and brought the ideas and statements to Mayor Harold Washington. The Alderman and Mayor, and then the City Council, discussed the need for the Parade and provided permission for the group to proceed with planning and then running the Chicago Vietnam Veterans WELCOME HOME Parade scheduled for June of 1986. The permission to go ahead was the catalyst to organize as the Chicago Vietnam Veterans Parade

Committee. Tom Stack set up the first meeting where it was decided that the following committees would be formed:

Honorary Chairman – Mayor Harold Washington of Chicago. The mayor appointed William Davis who became the focus of communication between our efforts and the mayor's office. Author's Note: Harold L. Washington was the 51st Mayor of the City of Chicago from 1983-1987. He served in World War II in the U.S. Army Air Corp as a Sargent from 1942-1945, Central and South Pacific.

Parade Chairman – Tom Stack. Reporting to Tom were the following Committees and Chairpersons:

Vice Chairs: William Davis, Constance Edwards, Philip Meyer, Kenneth Plummer.

City Resources Coordinator: Maude DeVictor.

Executive Board:

Col. Ken Plumer (Ret.) - TV Cable Co. Oak Park, IL., William Davis - City of Chicago, office of Mayor Washington. Constance Edwards - Vietnam Nurse, Phil Meyer - Vietnam Veteran & Vet Center Chicago, Chuck Fabing IRS Chicago - Finance, Mr. Nealis, Bradley, Gene Connell (General Counsel) Law Firm.

Executive Committees:

Blind Veterans – George Brummel.

Business Liaison – William Horne – Holiday Mart Inn Jefferies and Company.

Communications/Media – Bob Leonard.

Communications – John Wright.

Community/Volunteers – Julio Gonzales

Counsel – Nealis, Bradley, & Connell.

Disabled Veterans – Doug Stout.

Distribution – Out of State Liaison – Linda Gonzales.

8

Finance – Chuck Fabing

Fund Raising – Larry Langowski

Hospitality – Angelo Terrell

Medal of Honor – Sammy Davis, Carmel Harvey Family (Posthumous). Allen Lynch, Milton Olive III Family (Posthumous). Ken Stumps.

Office Manager – Jeff Harvey.

POW/MIA – Mary Carol Lemon.

Program – Roger McGill

Treasurer – Karen Harvey.

Standing Committees – a number of standing committees were formed included in this and the following chapter.

Larry Langowski –Finance Chairman – Vietnam Veteran U.S. Army 11th Armor Cavalry 1966 – 1969 – System Analyst with Illinois Bell – Married with one son Larry Jr. Has a Master's in Economics, MBA in Finance. Belonged to VVA Chapter #242 & Fox Valley VietNow. He lived on North side of Chicago.

Charles T. Fabing – member of the Finance Committee. U.S. Army as a SP/4, worked for the Internal Revenue Service, as a Team Coordinator – Large Case Programs – Coordinated the examination of large corporations which file tax returns. Charles lived on the South Side of Chicago, married with three children.

Constance Edwards –Vice-Chairman the Vietnam Veterans Parade Committee. Vietnam Veteran U.S. Army Nurse at the 24th Evacuation Hospital at Long Binh, as the Head Nurse. She left the Army as a Captain. She has a Master of Science degree in Public Health. She was the University Professor of Nursing at Governors State University, University Park, IL. She was also the Chief Nurse, 801st General Hospital in Chicago. She is married with two children.

Julio Gonzales –Outreach Chairman – Vietnam Veteran U.S. Army 173rd Airborne – June 1966. He majored in science and biology at the University of Illinois. He is with three children. He lived on the NW side of Chicago.

Roger McGill –Program Chairman – U.S. Army - Vietnam Veteran 3rd Squadron, 4th Cavalry, 25th Infantry Division, Cu Chi, Vietnam as a Cavalry Scout. He was a Manager at Illinois Bell Telephone Co. His college education was at Lewis College in Lockport, IL., and Montay College in Chicago, IL. He is married to Cathy with three children. He lives on the Northwest side of Chicago in the Mayfair community.

Eugene Connell, Jr. –Lawyer for the Parade Committee -- U.S. Air Force in the Air Command, 376th Bomb-Wing Intelligence NCO, Kadena AFB – 1968 – 1971. He is a Partner with Nealis Bradley & Connell Ltd. He holds a B.S. in Economics from Xavier University, MBA Management from Xavier University and a Doctor of Jurisprudence, Northern Illinois University. Eugene was General Counsel, City of Chicago, Office of Veterans Affairs, Legal Consultant, Illinois Attorney General Office of Veterans Advocacy.

Angelo Terrell – member of the Hospitality Committee. U.S. Navy 1972-1975. U.S.S. John Paul Jones D.D.G. 32 during Vietnam. Was the employed as Assistant State Director for Veterans Employment and Training U.S. Department of Labor. He is married with two children. He is a member of the DAV and VFW and American Legion.

Col. Kenneth A. Plummer -- member of the Executive Committee. U.S. Army (Ret) Served during Korea & Vietnam. Enlisted as a Private during WW II. Was an Infantry 2nd Lieutenant and served as a Platoon Leader and Infantry Company Commander. He owned his own cable company in Oak Park, IL. Military awards CIB, Silver Star, Bronze Star, and other service Medals.

Dennis Fox – member of the Executive Committee and POW/MIA committee. U.S. Army 135th Aviation Company at Dong Ba Thien, Vietnam. He also served in the U.S. Air Force with the Tactical Squadron at Cam Rahn Bay. He is also a trustee of the Illinois Veterans Memorial in Springfield, IL. He owns his own business on the South side.

Phil Meyer – a member of the Executive Committee. U.S. Army – 25th Infantry Division with the WOLFHOUNDS 1/27th Infantry at Cu Chi, Vietnam. He is married and has one child. Phil is also an outreach specialist and counselor for Vietnam era veterans. He has a degree in teaching and counseling.

Allen J. Lynch – member of the Executive Committee. U.S. Army 1st Cavalry, 12th Cavalry – he received the Congressional Medal of Honor for his actions in Vietnam, with the 1st Cavalry. He has a Bachelor of Science Degree in Health Administration from SIU. He is a member of the VFW, American Legion, AMVETS, Marine Corps League, and President of Vietnam Veterans of America Chapter #242 Chicago. He is married to Susan, and they have three children. He lives in Gurnee, IL. He began a career with the Vietnam Veterans Administration for 11 years. Then went to the Illinois Attorney General's Office in Chicago, IL. as the Chief of the Veterans Advocacy Division.

Paul J. Nealis – member of the Executive Board. U.S. Marine Corps Sergeant, Vietnam combat Veteran, is married to Jane and they have one child. He is a Partner with the Law Firm Nealis, Bradley & Connell Ltd. In Chicago, IL. on the South side. He was a former Chicago Police Sergeant/Detective, Patrol & Detective Division

Homicide Section. He attended Lewis University College of Law a Juris Doctor (J.D.); he also has a Bachelor of Arts (B.A.) Chicago State University. He was on the Executive Board of the WELCOME HOME Parade as a Lawyer.

Mary Carol Lemon – Chairwoman for the POW/MIA Committee. Mother of Lieutenant Colonel Jeffery C. Lemon – U.S. Air Force listed as Missing in Action in Laos since 1971. She is also the Illinois Coordinator of the National League of POW/MIA Families.

PARADE FOCUS: ALL INCLUSIVE

While the "woke" generation takes great pride in claiming rights to the term "inclusive", these authors can attest to the fact that "inclusive" began long ago -- in the last century, and decades earlier. In Vietnam, we fought side-by-side with every race representative of America. We defended one another, protected one another, and now today – decades later – care for one another. The Parade organizers with a strong focus on Tom Stack were adamant about the need for inclusion giving rise to "The Minority Connection of Veterans for the Chicago Vietnam Veterans WELCOME HOME Parade."

Tom personally reached out to all the different communities:

MAVA: In the Hispanic Community is MAVA (the Mexican American Veterans Association). They were very involved in every aspect of the parade ranging from working in the office to organizing their communities to come to the Parade.

Puerto Rican Veterans: The Puerto Rican community of Veterans helped in so many ways including serving on a range of different parade committees.

African American Veterans: There were many involved African American veterans with a high degree of participation:

Connie Edwards, a nurse in Vietnam, belonged to a group of nurses and women veterans on the South side. She was so helpful in leading their involvement as they become important members of the parade in ways including planning and participating as marchers.

Angello Terrell, the Hospitality Chairman of the parade, was very involved with Parade planning. His efforts generated the involvement of the African American Veterans to help with the parade and the various African American Veterans Organizations to march.

Col. Frank Marchant from the Monfort Point Marines held Parade planning meetings at their location on the South side of Chicago which we all attended. He focused on making sure African American Veterans that he knew would be coming to the parade and to help in any way that they could. This was very successful in encouraging attendance.

Adam Mendez Jr. – U.S. Army 1974. He worked for Social Security and is an Administrative Officer with a wide variety of responsibilities with the Social Security Administration. He also served as the commander of the 413th Replacement Detachment 86th USARCOM. He is Vice Commander of American Legion Post 38, which works with paralyzed veterans and their families. He is a member of IMAGE, the Federal Executive Board of the Hispanic Employment Subcommittee and Associate Director of the National Association of Hispanic American Officers.

CHAPTER THREE

An Incredible Volunteer Network

The authors acknowledge and want to share with our readers, that despite our best intentions it is very likely we unintentionally left out the names and efforts of individuals who were so instrumental to the success of this parade. Amassing 176,000 veterans is a large job. None of us had ever done this before. We had the spirit, the passion, and the will but we are not the same people who plan, orchestrate, and lead large national parade efforts. We were instead a large group of loosely woven together veterans who reached out by word of mouth and media presence. In the latter vein, people such as Bob Leonard, well-known radio personality and Vietnam Veteran and Jerry Taft, media weatherman and Vietnam veteran, were among the many in the media who were so helpful.

In this Chapter, we will do our best to call out those who helped make this event so successful. And, for those not called out, we apologize for the oversight. Many others are discussed in later chapters dealing with Fundraising, Chicago support, the Traveling Wall, and the actual day of the event. Please know, we were assembling decades old memories and notes and frankly we too have entered the "CRS" stage of life!

Parade Volunteers

Jim Stevens – The Traveling WALL at Grant Park

Harold Biechman – Disabled American Veterans

Jim Cepican – Veterans Foreign Wars

Jim McElveen – V.P. Diedarichs & Associates

William Dolan – Military Order of the Purple Hearts

16

Brian Duffy – Windy City Veterans

Diane Carlson Evans – Vietnam Woman's Memorial

John R. Fears – VA Edward Hines Hospital

Simeon Fleming – Office of State Guardian

Robert Healey – Chicago Police Marines

Thomas Hart – Citicorp

Joe Hertel – Vietnam Veterans of American Chapter #209

Eric Johnson – U.S. Post Office

Herb Johnson – Combined Veterans

Irv Kupcinet – Chicago Sun-Times

Christopher Lane – Vet Center

Ray Laurence – Incarcerated Vets

Chuck Lofrano – Entertainment Committee

John Mahoney – America Legion

Joseph Mannion – Catholic War Veterans

Robert Mitchler – Navy Club of the United States

Tom Moran – Veterans of Foreign Wars

Herman Herbert Moses – Jewish War Veterans

Ray Ney – Commander of Marine Corps League

Mickey O'Neill – American Ex-Prisoners of War

Samuel L. Parks – Veterans Employment and Training

A.S. Pate – Veterans Administration Edward Hines Hospital

Lee Perry – Air National Guard

Ed Rogers – VietNow

Scott Samuels – Chicago Convention & Visitors Bureau

Bob Scherbaum – Staley's Restaurant

Reggie Smith – Veterans Assistance Commission

Paul Stanford, Jr. VA Medical Center Director

John Steer – Minister – Vietnam Veteran

Ernest Stetz – Polish Legion of American Veterans

Ray Sullivan – Military Order of the Purple Heart Association

Barry Summers – Vietnam Veterans of America Chapter #153

Lam Tom – South Vietnamese Association

Carmen Trombetta – Italian American War Veterans

Walter "Gibby" Vartan – Brig. General U.S. Air Force Reserve

Bob Gibson – Australia Vietnam Veteran

Col. Frank Marchant – Monfort Point Marines

Profiles of Some Committee Members for the Chicago
Vietnam Veterans

WELCOME HOME Parade

Ellen Lally – member of the committee to encourage nurses to come to the parade. U.S. Army Nurse at the 3rd Field Hospital in Saigon, she met her husband Bob who was an Army Medic, in Vietnam and they live in Springfield, IL. and have one Daughter. When returning from Vietnam she was a Nurse in the ER in St. Mary's Hospital in Springfield, IL. At one time in Vietnam, she treated 25 patients at once.

AR Kail "Tunnel Rat" Giles – neighborhood Liasion and member of the communications committee. U.S. Army, Vietnam – he belongs to American Vietnam Veterans with P.U.S.H., VietNow, and Athletics for Christ.

Lam Tom – Committee to bring the Vietnamese people to the Parade.42nd Ranger Battalion 21st Infantry Division in Vietnam served in the South Vietnamese Armed Services. Lam and his family were among the last to board helicopters leaving the embassy. Came to the U.S. and worked at Olin Chemical division as Production Supervisor. Now his own businessman he is the owner of Mekong

Restaurant, Chicago. (See "A Lam Ton's American Dream", by Connie Lauerman, Chicago Tribune, January 1, 1989).

Chuck S. Lofrano – Entertainment Committee. Served in combat in Vietnam in 1968 as an M60 Infantry machine gunner with 3rd Battalion, 27th Marines and 3rd Battalion, 7th Marines. Received a disabling gunshot wound and was decorated eight times. Chuck was one of the organizers of the Parade, running the entertainment committee at the Grant Park Band shell.

Jeff Harvey – Volunteer organizing those who wanted to help. Jeff was the office manager at our office in the Xerox building downtown. He organized the volunteers calling in to ask what they could do to help. He spoke with Veterans calling in from all over the country trying to find out what they needed to do to come to the parade. The office was manned from 8 a.m. to 5 p.m. up until the days before the Parade. There was always work in the office with mailings and letters to be typed and sent to various business in Chicago. Fundraising as a key part of this effort. The phone lines never stopped ringing. Jeff led the volunteers who were instrumental in the success of the parade.

Jim Stevens - Volunteer organizing the group to help visitors find names on the traveling wall was a tremendous help with the Traveling Wall exhibit. He served with the U.S. Marine Corps in Vietnam in the Chu Lia area of Vietnam. He was married to Helen for many years, she was a schoolteacher at St. Edward grammar school NW side of the City of Chicago. Later she became a principle at St. Tars grammar school on the NW side of the City of Chicago. Jim was a security officer at Illinois Masonic Hospital for years, until he got sick from cancer related to Agent Orange which took his life at an early age. Jim set up a table for that and had his committee members post themselves. They walked the Traveling Wall asking people if they needed help in finding a name.

Jim Stevens, Harry Beyne III, John Wright, Larry Langowski, John Mahoney, Mike LaRocco, and Roger McGill, set up the Traveling Wall, one early morning when it arrived with John Devitt, who brought the Traveling Wall around the country for people that couldn't make it to Washington, D.C.

Program Committee Members

The following people were on the Program Committee, led by Roger Mc Gill and worked for over a year helping to organize the program part of the Parade.

We had the Order of March for the day of the Parade, The Food Vendors in Grant Park, The Reviewing Stands on LaSalle Street & Washington. The Traveling WALL on Michigan just before Grant Park, the Dance the night before the Parade at the Holiday Mart Inn., and numerous other jobs.

Every one of these volunteers, most of them Veterans, made outstanding contributions to the Program Committee.

THE BERWYN/CICERO Chapter of VietNow will march in the second position in the Friday, June 13, Vietnam Veterans Parade in Chicago. The parade position lottery committee includes (front row from left) Harry Beyne of Rocco of the parade committee; Tom Day, program secretary of the parade committee; and (back row) Jack Corcoran, junior vice commander of the Berwyn based Commodore Barry Post, American Legion; and Roger McGill, parade

Harry Beyne, Jim Hogan, John Mazzucchelli – Wayne Asnerud, Tim Abney, George Brummel, Rus Cearnecki, Mike LaRocco, Terry McDonald, Wayne & Linda Gehl, Gene Connell, Tom Day, Jackie Marx & Bob Carpenter, Dennis Fox, Linda Gonzales, Bob Hanley (see "the Main Event" for the vital contributions Bob made), Ken Pickering, Mike Landner, Mrs. Landner, John Corcoran, Bob Jones, Nacho Rodregiuz, The Parade Marshals, Margurite Tully, Helen Doran, Ann Rashford, Vietnow Berwyn-Cicero, VVA Chapter #242, VVA Chapter #209, VVA Chapter #153.

The National League of POW/MIA Families Efforts

The National League of POW/MIA Families was run by Ann Mills Griffiths. Her brother, Commander James M. Mills was with Fighter Squadron 21 on the USS Coral Sea and was in a Navy F4B aircraft which went down on 9/21/1966. He then was listed as Missing in Action (MIA) in Vietnam. (Note: the office of the National League of POW/MIA Families is located at 5673 Columbia Pike, Suite 100 Falls Church, VA but with chapters all over the country including one in Illinois).

In Illinois, Mary Carol Lemon of Flossmoor, IL. was that Chairwoman for the National League of POW/MIA Families. Her son, Jeffery Charles Lemon from Flossmoor, IL. was shot down over LAOS on April 25, 1971. Kien Hoa Province. He was a Lt. Col. In the U.S. Air Force and assigned to 7th Air Force 366th, 421st Tactical Squadron. He flew a F110. He was 28 years old when he was shot down. His remains were found at the site many years later and he is buried in Hawaii.

POW/MIA Service, June 14, 1986

Tom Stack wanted to make sure that Mary Carol Lemon was the Chairwoman for the POW/MIA Service that would be held at the Daley Center on Saturday June 14th, 1986, at 11:00 a.m., it was also Flag Day. She was the Chairwoman fully helped by a committee of Veterans. Dennis Fox was her righthand person in helping her plan this event.

For the Service, there was a stage, set up with flowers, a speaker platform, and POW/MIA Flags. In attendance on the stage were a number of others including Jerry Taft a news weatherman in Chicago, who was also an Air Force Pilot in Vietnam. Jerry flew Jets, on many missions in Vietnam, and was one of the keynote speakers that morning. In addition, there were other POW/MIA families from Illinois, and they spoke at this event also about their family members.

Carol Walters, also a POW/MIA wife as her husband Tim Walters was MIA for a number of years. He was in a MAC-SOG Unit in Vietnam. He was up in a piper cub airplane with the pilot of that aircraft, doing the spotting for his group of MAC-SOG soldiers on the ground. The NVA spotted the plane and shot it down. Tim and the Pilot were MIA for years until, some years ago, his and the Pilot's remains were found. They were identified in Hawaii at the joint resolution performing DNA testing on the bones received. Carol had his remains buried in his hometown of Niles MI. Carol worked for many years here in Chicago on POW/MIA issues. She would always march with the POW/MIA banner and Vietnam Veterans. Some years ago, she moved to Arizona where she subsequently passed away.

CHAPTER FOUR

Thank You – City of Chicago and Its Businesses

Source of Photo: CherriesWriter, Vietnam War Website

From Mayor Washington's office to the solid and profoundly helpful efforts of Alderman Bernie Stone to the Greater State Street Council to a number of City of Chicago personnel, police officers and business leaders, the helping hands of Chicago were fully extended to Vietnam veterans. So many contributed to the ability to organize, fund, promote and provide the logistics for the Welcome Home parade. This chapter could, by itself, be an entire book. Unfortunately, we lack the details to call out the names and efforts of all those who helped. This Chapter provides only a glimpse into the City's efforts on behalf of Vietnam Veterans. Our gratitude was then, is now, and will forever be extended to these wonderful individuals representing the City of Chicago and to those businesses and business leaders who stepped up to support the efforts.

The Devil is in The Details....

From food vendors to crowd control to porta potties, the details for an event this size as enormous. Roger was chair of the

Program Committee and shares these insights: Whenever I think of the "go to" person for the city, I think of Marguerite Tully.

Marguerite Tully – City of Chicago Special Events – 1979 – 1991. Marguerite worked for Mrs. Louis Weisberg who was the Director of Special Events for the City of Chicago at the time of the Parade.

When I needed something, as I and my fellow committee members so often did, she was there to give me the contacts or advise who to call. These contacts ranged from any Department in the City to outside contractors with whom she had worked on various events including food vendors for the event after the Parade in Grant Park.

One such contact was Tom C. Corcoran – *National Restaurant Association*, who had set up the Vendors for the Taste of Chicago. I asked one of the Program Committee members, a 134 electrician, to contact him regarding food vendors. This individual wasn't comfortable doing this on his own, so he set an appointment with Tom and me. We met with Tom and discussed what we were looking for; Tom wrote up the budget and what he could do. Tom Stack was concerned about costs and asked our attorney Eugene (Gene) Connell to call me. I explained to him the plan; he went back to Tom, and it then was all settled: we had a person who would set up the stands and get the food vendors to provide the food to sell, just as with the Taste of Chicago.

Marguerite Tully then provided support in another 'highly needed' area. We needed a LARGE number of Porta Potties in Grant Park. Marguerite provided the contact information for the porta potty company the city worked with for the Taste of Chicago. We had a city lunch meeting to discuss what was needed, where. They provided the bid for the event, and I presented it to Tom Stack and the Executive Committee, and it was accepted.

Marguerite helped me with so other issues and through this process, we discovered a family connection. Her Uncle and cousins were from St. Edward parish on the NW side of Chicago. Of course, as is so often the case with Chicago neighborhoods, we knew one another.

As expected, an event of this magnitude requires tremendous logistic support and that means help and support from the Chicago police and their efforts to coordinate with area businesses. This is where Pete Schurla – Chicago Police Department Commander Special Events for the City of Chicago was so helpful. Pete attended many meetings about the different events that were going to take place during the Chicago Vietnam Veterans WELCOME HOME PARADE. One primary focus was the Parade itself and the Order of March from Navy Pier to Grant Park.

At one of our meetings, Roger was asked to call the person in charge of the Chamber of Commerce for Michigan Avenue to advise him that the Parade would progress down Michigan Avenue from Ontario Street to Wacker Drive. The planned route was to come over from Navy Pier, turn North on Rush Street and then turn onto Ontario, to Michigan -- going around the Marriott Hotel at that location. This was not happy news to the Chamber. Roger was advised it would tie up the businesses on Michigan Ave. Roger, in turn, advised this was a courtesy call.

He then called Commander Schurla and advised that the Chamber leader was 'unhappy.' Commander Schurla asked, "Roger what can we do about this to put out the fire?" The answer to that question was a reroute go straight on Grand Avenue from Navy Pier to State Street, take State Street to Wacker Drive and Wacker over to LaSalle Street, and LaSalle down to Jackson and then over to the bandshell at Grant Park. The Commander asked if this would work for the Veterans, and Roger said, "Yes Sir, I do." Like that, a new plan was hatched. Commander Schurla did the rest by running with the ball for the change. At that time, no one ever knew of the change in the march except for Roger and Pete until the reasons were communicated to Tom Stack. Commander Schurla was a real pleasure to work with and a true leader in the Chicago Police Department.

Jim Hogan –Chicago Policeman --worked in the 14th Police District for some years. He was a partner with Carlos Saladino also in the 14th Police District. They rode together for a year. During this time, they talked about many things, but neither ever mentioned they were Vietnam Veterans, nor did they mention that they served in the same U.S. Army Division – 25th Infantry at Cu Chi, Vietnam. Jim with the 1/5th Mech, and Carlos with the WOLFHOUNDS. But at the Chicago WELCOME HOME Parade when they saw each other downtown the day of the Parade they both said at the same time together "What are you doing here?"

During the year of parade planning, Jim transferred to 11th & State Police Headquarters. He became involved with parade planning and was on the Program Committee. During this time, Jim ran the mail room of the CPD. This was so helpful to the Parade Committee when we were sending out the mailing list to Veteran Organizations and Veterans all across the county. Jim understood how the lists had to be sorted, lined up and ordered for the Post Office. He then would take them and mail them, greatly expediting the process for us. (Note: Linda and Julio Gonzales' home – their dining room, kitchen, and living room – became a mail sorting station for the parade efforts).

Carlos Saladino was a neighbor of Roger's living in the Mayfair Area on the NW side of Chicago. He and Roger knew one another from growing up in our neighborhood, and his children also went to St. Edward Grammar school. Two of them today are Chicago Policemen. Another one was a Combat Medic and Airborne Ranger and did a few tours in Iraq/Afghanistan. His other son is an Iron worker. After the Chicago Vietnam Veterans WELCOME HOME Parade, Carlos has become very involved with the Chicago Police Department dealing with a number of Veteran issues. Through his efforts, many of them have been able to receive the benefits to which they are entitled from their time in Vietnam and the service. Carlos, today, still provides this support. He has authored many articles in the Chicago FOP magazine for Veterans and is well known in the CPD for helping Policeman who are Veterans.

CHAPTER FIVE

Leading Up to the Main Event

With an event of this magnitude, our oft-used term "the devil is in the details" is absolutely true. There were so many efforts associated with the ability to march including press, signage, arranging for the traveling wall, helping out-of-area veterans, gatherings prior to the parade, and setting forth the program. This chapter provides information on a 'smattering' of these events and those people who were essential to the program and operations.

Paying the Bills!

One avenue for money was the patch itself. Julio Gonzales said, "Let's get to Midwest Swiss Embroidery 5590 N. Northwest Highway and see what kind of patch they can make for us for the WELCOME HOME PARADE." Roger and Julio talked to John Mazzucchelli, one of the brothers who owned the company and who was also a Vietnam Veteran who served with the U.S. Army, 5th Infantry Division up at the DMZ in Vietnam. Additionally, Roger discovered that John's Sister-in-Law Dott, and her husband, John's brother had lived right across the street from him when he was growing up. They owned a building that had a store on the first floor, and they lived in the back of the store.

We told John we wanted a patch we to sell everyone attending the Parade. His design was a patch of the State of Illinois, done in the blue background, with the City of Chicago in gold and a gold star that representing the location of Chicago in the State. Across the middle of the patch was WELCOME HOME in gold letters, and below that, the Vietnam Service Ribbon in its full color. Just about everyone at the parade bought one. At John's recommendation, we also sold blue hats with the patch

There were multiple fundraising efforts occurring to pay for the Parade with many volunteers involved. The State Street Council, and its representative businesses were involved; the Playboy Foundation though Mike Carr, a Vietnam veteran, made a generous donation, and Vietnam Veterans were also significant contributors. Flyers such as this were key in bringing in people for contributions and for events such as those on May 10, May 12, and May 15.

"Two vets who are executives with Jefferies and Co. Inc., a brokerage firm at 55 W. Monroe St., called and offered a vacant suite in their offices. Thus, without any money, the committee acquired a posh office with four telephones at a toney address. Early on the committee members thought they could do the whole show for $1.5 million. They hoped to attract large corporate donations but never raised more than $300,000. The city promised $75,000 in seed money to get them started but dragged its feet until March 1986, before releasing the first $25,000. ``. (Source and for further information see, "At Peace at Last: After 11 Years and an Emotional Parade, Vietnam Vets Finally Feel Welcome" by William Mullen, Chicago Tribune Magazine 8/17/86).

The Traveling Wall

Jim Stevens was a tremendous help with the Traveling Wall exhibit (See Chapter 3 Volunteers). As Roger relates, Jim came down to the office downtown and met with Tom Stack and Roger McGill. He was willing to run the group of volunteers that wanted to help people find the names on the Traveling Wall in Grant Park Area. This was a big effort. It required day and night effort for the one full week when the Traveling Wall was in Chicago. He set up a schedule for those that would help and had a couple of books with all the names of those that were KIA in Vietnam. Those volunteers under Jim's guidance helped family members, Veterans, and others looking for names on the Traveling Wall that they either knew from schools or their neighborhoods. Jim set up a table for that and had his committee members post themselves. They walked the Traveling Wall asking people if they needed help in finding a name.

Jim Stevens, Harry Beyne III, John Wright, Larry Langowski, John Mahoney, Mike LaRocco, and Roger McGill, set up the Traveling Wall, one early morning when it arrived with John Devitt, who brought the Traveling Wall around the country so people that couldn't make it to see the Wall in person, could do so locally.

Every Veteran who helped set up the wall found it very emotional taking the panels off of John Devitt's truck and carrying

them to the set-up location. We placed the panels in order, and then, under John's guidance, we set up everything and held them in place. It was a very emotional event.

Years later – March 29, 2021 – Vietnam Veterans Day is honored in Chicago at the permanent memorial to the over 3,000 Veterans from Illinois killed in Vietnam on the River Walk. Pictured are Carlos Saladino and Roger McGill at the March 29th event, representing VVA Chapter 242.

Setting the Stage for the Line Up

Roger McGill – Mike LaRocco (a U.S. Marine Vietnam Veteran and History Professor at St. Francis College in Joliet, IL) and many other committee members of the Program Committee, bought ½" x 6' high poster board to make signs. The signage was to portray all the Divisions and Units of the U.S. Army, U.S. Marines, U.S. Navy, U.S. Air Force, the Seebees, the U.S. Coast Guard and literally every Association and Veterans Organization that signed up for the Parade including but not limited to:

173rd Airborne Association	4th Infantry Division
25th Infantry Division, Special Forces	1st Aviation
199 LIB, the 1st Cavalry	American
82nd Airborne Division	11th Armor Cavalry
DAV	Windy City Veterans
VVA	MAVA
VFW	Monfort Point Marines
AL	Jewish War Veterans
AMVETS	VVAW
Purple Hearts	Gold Star Mothers
IDVA	Congressional Medal of Honor Society
75th Rangers	Ex POW Association

101st Infantry Division	Vietnam Women's Memorial Project
Air Mobile	And many other Veterans Organizations from across the country
PAV	
VIETNOW	

The day before the parade, committee members came to Navy Pier. Now in 1986, this was not the Navy Pier of today. The middle of Navy Pier was open and had a walkway around and above the floor of Navy Pier. The Committee brought cable ties and headed up that walkway with its surrounding railing. They took the 1/2" lumber with the poster board attached with staples and tied them with the cable ties up to the railings.

Their posters set the stage for the line ups so those coming to the Parade knew where to line up on the day of the Parade. This took the Committee a couple of hours as there were many who had signed up to come to the WELCOME HOME Parade. To celebrate our efforts, they then went out to eat and have a few drinks!

Vietnam veterans have come a LONG way since the 1986 Parade. The Vietnam Veterans Memorial was dedicated on November 11, 2005. It features a rectangular fountain basin and stone wall inscribed with the names of those who died during the Vietnam War. According to the Smithsonian Institution: "This memorial is dedicated to veterans from all branches of the armed services who served in Vietnam. It replaces the former Vietnam Memorial located on Wacker Drive that was dedicated on November 11, 1982. The inscribed stones from that memorial have been incorporated into the plaza of this memorial." The featured sculpture was created by Gary Tillery, himself a Vietnam veteran (Wikipedia).

Getting the Word Out

The City of Chicago really was behind this Parade. From the Mayor's office to the individual on the street, Chicago worked to inspire and promote. Chicago Media and individual representatives were so helpful to this effort. The effort was greatly helped by Vietnam Veterans who themselves were media members.

Irv Kupcinet, Jerry Taft, Bob Leonard were just a few examples of media support. It was Bob Leonard, radio personality, who said the day of the parade changed his life.

It was William Mullen (Chicago Tribune) who wrote an excellent article (Source and for Further Information See, "At Peace at Last: After 11 Years and an Emotional Parade, Vietnam Vets Finally Feel Welcome" by William Mullen, Chicago Tribune Magazine 8/17/86) recapping so many of the moments leading to and the day of the event.

And it was Anne Keegan (born 1943 and passed away May 18, 2011) who made a significant impact in the ability to bring in veterans from Hines VA Hospital. Here is this story as related by Roger Mc Gill:

"Anne Keegan – Chicago Tribune Columnist and the wife of Leonard Aronson who worked for WTTW Channel 11 was a tremendous help. I found this quote about Anne Keegan: "Arguably the best female reporter/writer in the history of Chicago Journalism, Anne Keegan was ferocious, feisty, and passionately devoted to her craft. In short, she was an original."

I saw this firsthand on a Saturday at one of our weekly update meetings at our office at the Xerox building.

Tom Stack would lead the meeting and then we all gave our reports on how things were progressing in our committees. After we all gave our reports she asked, if any of us were having any problems getting things done, or people being committed to the Parade we were planning.

I spoke up and told her I was having a problem with the Director of Hines VA Hospital at this time. I had called him and asked if he would plan to have buses take the Veterans at Hines VA Hospital so they could ride in those buses at the front of the Parade. He told me in no uncertain terms he was not going to do that. Anne asked me for his name telephone number.

Scant time had passed when Anne called the Director of Hines VA Hospital and talked to him about my request. She told him in no uncertain terms that if he didn't comply, she would write an article about him and what he was not willing to do for the Veterans in Hines Hospital.

The Director of Hines VA Hospital called me to say we here at Hines will do whatever is needed to have the Veterans on the buses and in the Chicago Vietnam Veterans WELCOME HOME Parade."

Behold the power of the press and particularly Anne Keegan!

Flash Forward to Today: It is with great appreciation that the authors acknowledge the efforts and support of Jackie Bange, an American Award-winning Journalist working for WGN News at Nine. She joined WGN – TV News in August 1993. Jackie and WGN – TV News have been consummate supporters of Veterans and particularly those efforts associated with Vietnam Veterans. providing coverage at key commemorative events such as the dedication of the Vietnam War Memorial Wall, Memorial Day ceremonies and activities acknowledging those who have served. On behalf of all Veterans, we thank Jackie and WGN – TV as well as so many other members of Chicago media (Chicago Tribune, Chicago

Sun-Times, and local affiliates of NBC, CBS, ABC, WTTW) for their support of American patriots.

CHAPTER SIX

The Main Event

Time to Party in Anticipation

The night before the Chicago Vietnam Veterans WELCOME HOME Parade, there was a Veterans Dance at the Holiday Mart Inn, on the top floor in the main ball room. Most of the Committee members and other Veterans and Organizations that knew about it attended.

Tim Abney a Vietnam Veteran who was a DJ played the music for the night: all music from the 60's & 70's. Tim also was a very well-known DJ in Vietnam with a Saigon-based radio station that played throughout South Vietnam.

Not only did the veterans have the dance that night, but they also held a raffle to raise money for any program that was necessary for Veterans after the parade. That night when the raffle was held after all the tickets were sold, the following people were on the stage holding the raffle: Ellen Lally a Nurse that served at an Evac Hospital in Vietnam, Tim Abney, Bob Kolling – 1st Cavalry in Vietnam and myself Roger McGill. I would call out the winning numbers after Ellen, Bob, or Tim would pick them.

Tim Abney now lives in AZ. Ellen Lally and her husband Bob – a Medic in Vietnam live in Springfield, IL. Bob Kolling who lived in Naperville, IL. has since passed away from Agent Orange Problems. He has also lost one of his legs due to an injury he sustained in Vietnam years earlier. The picture below was taken the night before the Chicago Vietnam Veterans WELCOME HOME Parade at the Holiday Mart Inn on Orleans Street. We had a sock hop, with a DJ that night, and we also sold raffle tickets and raffled off prizes.

In the picture Roger McGill calling off a winning number, Ellen Lally – from Springfield, IL. who was an Evac Nurse in Vietnam, Tim Abney who was the DJ for the evening and who also worked Arm Forces Radio in Saigon, Vietnam which was broadcast to the Soldier's all over Vietnam, and Bob Kolling (background) who was with the 1st Cavalry in Vietnam and was on the Parade Committee. He has since passed from Agent Orange.

Also, earlier that evening at the Holiday Mart Inn, the Medal of Honor Society held their dinner. AL Lynch a CMOH – 1st Cavalry – 12th Cavalry, who worked for the Illinois Attorney General, Neal Harritgan, as the Veterans Advocate and other CMOH Veterans were in attendance – Sammy Davis – 9th Infantry Division, Ken Stump – 25th Infantry Division, and family members of KIA CMOH Milton Olive III, the family of KIA CMOH Carmel Harvey.

The start of the March of the Vietnam Veterans WELCOME HOME Parade

MIKE LaRocco was a U.S. Marine Vietnam Veteran, and a History Professor at St. Francis College in Joliet, IL. Roger McGill provides the following:

The Day of the Chicago Vietnam Veterans WELCOME Parade, we stayed overnight at the Holiday Mart Inn and about 9 a.m. Tom Stack called me and said let's head down to the lobby and we will take the Limo over to the start of the parade. The lineup of the parade was going OK, but there were more and more Veterans and family members coming to Navy Pier. It was decided to move some of the Units up out of Navy Pier so there would be more room for those still coming.

At the front of the parade were all the Committee members and their families. Gen. Westmoreland was also there, as well as some other special guests that were invited to march with us. One of them was a Vietnam Veteran, in a wheelchair, who was from the Western Suburbs, he had saved, a few days earlier, a little girl near his home who went into a swimming pool and was drowning. He got out of his wheelchair and into the pool and pulled her out. It was all over the news and Tom wanted this Vietnam Veteran and his family to be recognized the day of the Parade. They were.

The parade kicked off at 10 a.m. and by the time the last Units in the Parade reach the Grant Park Band Shell it was three hours later. We had figured that it would take about an hour or so, but with all those   that   who   attended   lasted   a   lot   longer.

Bob Weiland, U.S. Army Medic, 25th Infantry Division, lost his legs in Vietnam at CuChi. Following Bob are members of the Parade Committee with their families.

There were actually 176,000 Vietnam Veterans that marched in the Parade. Along the Parade route there were construction workers who were cheering us on; there were people in business who came out to the streets and cheered us on. All were saying WELCOME HOME. When we hit State Street and turned South heading to Wacker Drive there were more people on the street saying the same things, some coming off the sidewalks and giving hugs and saying Thank You & Welcome Home. There were even Veterans who were standing on the sidewalks, and when other Veterans marching in the parade, told them to come on and join in the parade. Many of them did.

We headed over Wacker Drive to LaSalle Street. The scene looking down LaSalle Street was unreal; it was sidewalk to buildings on both sides of the street with people cheering us on. Then from every one of the buildings south of the Lake Street Elevated, people were in windows of every building hanging out the windows throwing confetti and yelling at the top of their lungs WELCOME HOME, some had signs saying, "WE LOVE YOU".

When all the Veterans passed the Reviewing stand on LaSalle and Washington, with Gen. Westmoreland in the stands then, all the Units passing by stopped to salute him and he saluted back.

> "All the Parade Committee was at the front of the Parade leading it off that morning. Bob Weiland who was a Medic with the 25th Infantry Division and lost both of his legs was leading us off, he had walked across the country from CA. – to NY., on these pads he had made and with big pads on his hands, he walked that way from the start of the parade to Grant Park leading the way. We all had our families with us and that was as special two of my children were able to walk and my youngest was being pushed by Cathy my wife, in a type of buggy that they had for young children. It was just amazing that day, and we all walked until we reached the reviewing stands on LaSalle and Washington. Some of those went into the reviewing stands where the Mayor Washington, and the Governor Thompson the announcer of the parade. My wife and I and the children went to the reviewing stand right across from it on the West side of LaSalle Street. My oldest son said to me Dad what are you going to do now. I said when the 25th Infantry Division come by I am getting out of the Reviewing stand and marching the rest of the way to Grant Park with them. My wife Cathy, my daughter Colette and James my youngest I told to meet us at Grant Park Band Shell where I had other things to do, and they did." Roger McGill

The Parade then marched all the way down LaSalle Street to Jackson Blvd. and made a left turn and headed to Grant Park Band Shell. The Units split up, some stayed at the Band Shell to listen to the Bands that would be playing the rest of the afternoon and evening. The Food Vendors were selling their food to all that wanted to eat.

42

Many of the hotel's on Michigan Ave. and some of the side streets all had hospitality rooms, and hundreds of hundreds of Veterans and their families went to them to meet other Veterans that some had not seen for years.

To say it was an awesome day would be an understatement. The easiest way to say what happened that day is that we were all WELCOMED HOME by the City of Chicago that we all love and live in to this day. Thank You Chicago then and now.

And They Came from Around the World

The Australians were among the 176,000 Veterans marching. From Left to Right: Johnny "JW" Wilson, Barry Dowset, Robert Dodds, Peter Poulton, Bob "Bomber" Gibson. (Source: Vietnam Veterans Parade Chicago – 1986. Photographs by Tom Conroy, Text by Kris Colt. Page 65). Also, in attendance Lachlan Irvine.

Retired Gen. William Westmoreland, who commanded U.S. forces in Vietnam, served as grand marshal for the parade, which unlike two similar parades in New York was open to veterans of all eras and their families.

On the bill for two days of music in Grant Park were Dennis DeYoung, a former member of the rock band Styx, and veterans' favorites like Britt Small and Festival. Comedian Bob Hope was invited but could not attend.

The city has provided sponsorship, resources and some funds, and United Air Lines and Amtrak offered reduced rates for travelers to the city, as did nearly 50 area hotels where many veterans stayed.

But it was Stack, a criminal justice teacher at Richard J. Daley Community College and holder of two Silver Stars and three Bronze Stars, who made his own dream come true by volunteering about 90 hours of work each week to organize the parade.

Source: "Chicago to Host Largest Vietnam Veterans Welcome Home Parade" by James Litke, June 7, 1986, Associated Press

``Hey! Westy's here!`` ``Look! It's Westmoreland!`` ``The old man came!`` And invariably each unit, each clump of men and women, stopped in front of the reviewing stand to cheer the old general. Whatever their personal feelings about Westmoreland may have been, he has become such a lightning rod for criticism of his war- -and their war--that a real sense of sympathy seems to have grown between him and his ex-troops. Most of the units that stopped to salute Westmoreland lingered until the parade's public-address announcer pleaded for them to move on, to keep the procession moving. Source: Chicago Tribune, "At Peace at Last: After 11 Years and An Emotional Parade, Vietnam Vets Finally Feel Welcome" by William Mullen, June 10, 2011

44

Parade Highlights

Vietnam Veterans from Roger Mc Gill's neighborhood: Pat Stacks Brother-in-Law, Dick Ashline U.S. Army Veteran, Pat Stack Seabee with the Marines in Vietnam, Art Bresnaham Marine Helicopter pilot in Vietnam Da Nang, Tim Stack U.S. Marine 1/9 in Cu Lia Vietnam and also Pat's brother, Bob Lobacz U.S. Army 4th Infantry Division Vietnam:

The Chicago Police Department Emerald Society Pipe & Drum Band featuring Chicago policemen. The one on the right is Jim Healy (Navy Vietnam Veteran deceased 2021.

Roger's wife Cathy, daughter Colette, not pictured but attending, his oldest son and youngest, son James. Roger and his family were on the Reviewing Stand across the street from Mayor

Washington, and then Governor Thompson. His oldest son said, "what are you going to do now?" Roger said "when the 25th Infantry Division comes by I am getting out of the stand and marching the rest of the way to Grant Park with them. I'll meet you there!

Navy Pier on the inside as former Vietnam Veterans came to the parade to line up. You can see the 1x2s up on the walkway with the name of the Units and information on where to line up below.

(Source: Vietnam Veterans Parade Chicago – 1986. Photographs by Tom Conroy, Text by Kris Colt. Pages 63 and 17).

Playboy not only provided funding they provided parade support. Author Harry Beyne is in the left background holding the banner. (Source: Vietnam Veterans Parade Chicago – 1986. Photographs by Tom Conroy, Text by Kris Colt).

CHAPTER SEVEN

What the Veterans Attending Had to Say

Hearing from some of the Veterans Who Attended....

JOHN B. ANDRES, JR. BCO 1/503 Infantry 173rd Airborne Brigade 1969-1970. "In 1986 when word got out that there was going to be a parade in Chicago to welcome home Vietnam

Veterans, I wasn't much interested. After all I returned from Vietnam in January 1970 – 16 years earlier. A fellow veteran and friend, Carlos Saladino called and asked if I was going to the Parade? No way was my answer. As the days got closer to June 13, 1986, there were some tributes going on around Chicago. One of these was the Moving Vietnam Wall. Carlos attended the moving wall ceremony in Grant Park.

He called me that night and was very emotional and asked if I would go with him to the parade for some support because we served together in Vietnam with the 173rd Airborne Brigade. I reluctantly said "Yes" I would go. We headed to Navy Pier Friday morning. The closer we got we saw more and more Vietnam Vets dressed in military fatigues. The crowds swelled and as we walked into Navy Pier it was a sea of Vets all in fatigues and military uniforms. I was blown away. After meeting a few old friends, the Parade kicked off.

We marched with our units. When we turned onto LaSalle Street you could see the amount of people lining the street to welcome us home. A surreal moment, after 16 years someone…a stranger…said "welcome Home"! Probably one of the best days of my life."

DAN HUFFMAN, I vividly remember our homecoming parade. We were ready for this. The atmosphere downtown was amazing. It was a perfect summer day. The crowds were great and welcoming. I remember the "hard hats" waving flags as we walked by. Being back with our brothers was an experience not forgotten. I carried my 2 ½ year old son on my shoulders. I felt proud to be a part of the parade and still proud of my service in Vietnam and proud for all those who served, especially those names on the wall.

BOB HANLEY, U.S. Marine Veteran – Bob was a Ret. Lt. Chicago Police Department and had been on Mayor Daley's police Detail and had been in charge of that. Bob was also a U.S. Marine

Veteran and had lots of experience doing things in the City of Chicago in his positions as a policeman, a Sgt., and Lt. for the Chicago Police Department. He was asked if he would be willing to be the head Marshall of the Parade and would he get Chicago Policemen to Volunteer to be Marshall's along the Parade route and at the start of the Parade at Navy Pier. He took on that responsibility and did a very good job of organizing those Parade Marshall's they all had banners across their chest that said Parade Marshall, they controlled the crowds coming into Navy Pier and helped people where to go and line up as they all had the maps we made up of where the Organizations were at inside Navy Pier, and they would direct them where to go.

Like everything else there were some things that happened that morning with the lineup of the parade. Bob was up front with me at Navy Pier, and when I saw things weren't going smoothly with the Veterans and their families going into the Pier to line up, "I said to Bob, we have to get these people back into the middle of the Pier, and also on the South side of that building where there were more line up spaces. So, we can get the Parade to move in order when we start moving." He said to me "Rog come with me, and I want to show you something." So, we walked down to where the entrance to Navy Pier was, and as we walked inside, there was nothing but wall to wall people and they were standing where the signs we put up the day before, and it was shoulder to shoulder in there. So, then we walked to the south outside of Navy Pier and it was the same thing there. The Parade was taking a life of its own and the crowd of Veterans was just very big to say the least and more and more Veterans were walking in. So, the two of us went back up front and said to each other looks like that is all we can do.

Just a note here after walking down there a van pulled up to the front where we were at. I went over to the van as it had stopped and I saw that there was a Veteran driving it, so I went to the passenger side window and said you have to move this van. He said where can I park it? I looked in the window and this Veteran had lost both his legs in Vietnam, and at that moment I said to him park it where every you can.

PETE KUKURBA U.S. Marine Corps – Vietnam Veteran Force Recon – 1968 – 1969. I was Recon Marine in Vietnam 1968 – 1969. I got on the L on Montrose on the Northside, got off at Grand Ave, got on the Bus going East. I saw bikes and carriages, like you would see in Saigon. I had a Flashback from the past, this was the day before the parade June 12th, 1986. They had the Moving Wall of the Vietnam Veterans, like the one in Washington, D.C., in Grant Park. I met Mr. Badsing, his son was the earliest Marine Vietnam Veteran from Chicago that was KIA. The family was from St. Edward Parish in Mayfair, on the Northside. We went to the Americana Congress Hotel on Michigan Ave. This was the Marine Corps Headquarters. I spent the night there, and the next day the Marine Corps Reserve Unit from the Northside 24th Marines, had a six-by truck to take us to Navy Pier. All Branches were gathering there. First time I was wearing my metals since the service. Veterans were coming from everywhere. My wife Stephanie brough my son and daughter there. My son Michael was 7 years old, and my daughter Carolyn was 10 years old. The Confetti on LaSalle Street was coming from the buildings, what a sight to see.

CHUCK LOFRANO, who ran the entertainment committee came to it with a strong background as a song writer and recipient of a Gold album. He had also worked with such artists as: Dennis De

Young (his brother-in-law), Frankie Valli, Roy Clark, Rich Little, Danny Gans, and Lina Eder. He Organized all the entertainment at the Grant Park Band Shell, which was done at the end of the Welcome Home Parade.

Chuck was married to Dennis De Youngs sister and in 2008 they had been married for thirty-eight years. Also, in 2008 long after the Chicago Welcome home parade he wrote a book IN SPITE OF IT ALL – it was his way for his children and grandchildren to know what he did in Vietnam, and what he did for the Welcome Parade in Chicago, IL. On June 13th, 1986. He did a very good job at what he did that day with the entertainment, one entertainer after another that day.

Chuck has since passed from Agent Orange which took his life from Cancer. This happened when he and others were planning a 25-year Reunion of the Chicago Vietnam Veterans Welcome Home Parade. His daughter picked up the baton after her father passed.

Bob Runtz: Spec 5

Date: Monday, March 22, 2021, 02:31 PM CDT

Lance & Roger

Per our Vet Meeting on Tuesday, here is a short story on my experience on that day.

When I came back from Nam no one on the plane wanted to sit next to me. I took off my uniform when I got home and never put it on again, much to my Mom's disappointment the first time taking her to church. My children were in their middle teens when they found out I had even been in service, let alone over to Nam. I was working for the phone company in the Engineering department in downtown Chicago in 1986. No one in my office of 75 people even had a clue that I was a Vet, except for a friend who had been in the Air Force.

I had served as radio support for the 11th Cav from Oct of 1966 to Oct 1967. We were a gypsy outfit who did not even have a unit patch. When the company got back back home, it was disbanded and the group became the Americal Division. I never felt like I belonged or had seen enough combat to march that day. My Air Force friend talked me into going down to the parade. I walked with the Americal group for about 1/2 mile but none of old group were in it. On the way to the office, I spotted Chris Noel (B movie actress and the voice of arm forces radio.) riding in a convertible. I had great respect for her support of our troops that still continues today. I stepped in the street and saluted her. To my surprise, she told her driver to stop, stood up in the car and saluted me and told me thank you for your service and welcome home. For the first time in 20 years, I felt a huge pride and a spring in my step heading back to the office.

SPEC 5 Bob Runtz

May 10, 2021 --- Letter from Carole Morrison regarding her husband
ROG MORRISON

First and foremost, a most sincere "thank you" from me to all of you for your service and dedication to this country of ours!!

Referencing the "Welcome Home Parade" for Vietnam Veterans, Jun

13, 1986, a Friday, held in Chicago ....my husband, Roger Morrison, whom I did NOT know while in the Army, 1966-1968, was very resistant to attend said parade!!

I told Roger, "Honey, I want to go.... I didn't know you while you were in the Army, and I'm not giving up!! (Rog was honorably discharged in April of 1968.... we met in June of that year.... just two months after discharge! Fast forward to 1986......I was UNRELENTING in my pursuit of attending the Welcome Home Parade! I also wanted to see the "Visiting Wall" of which I had heard about. I still had my prisoner

of war bracelet for a Major Claxton, who was MIA, and wanted to see if his name was on the wall.

Rog, begrudgingly, went into the attic of our home to retrieve his "Fatigue Shirt". (That's Roger, in one of the pictures enclosed, wearing said shirt!!) So, now that we have completely missed the parade timewise, we drove down to Grant Park, where all were gathered post-parade, and proceeded to walk into said park. I can close my eyes, and "see" what happened next.... Upon walking into Grant Park, another veteran, whom we did not know, walking out of Grant Park, saw Roger's rank of E6, saluted, and said, "Sergeant"!! I dissolved into tears and must admit that was my demeanor throughout the remainder of our day there!!

While walking around Grant Park, and chatting with various individuals, Rog happened to run into a fellow vet, V.C. Jackson, who, at that time, worked at the B&O Railroad where Roger was also employed. Jackson, pictured with Rog, served two tours in Vietnam.... was wounded twice while in the line of duty, and, deservedly so, received two Purple Heart. I was, and still am to this very day, so very proud of Roger's service!! He's, my hero!!! Carole Morrison, Roger's VERY PROUD wife!!!!)
(Roger Morrison and V.C. Jackson)

HARRY BEYNE, 101st Airborne Division, Vietnam. I met up with the VVA 242 and Ed Eich and I carried this large Chapter 242 banner through the entire parade. My wife and two children (ages 4 and 1) joined the sea of spectators in the Loop; it meant so much for me to see them there and the emotion of that time. It was exhilarating to see so many people welcoming Veterans home and to see the construction workers stopping work to clap and wave flags. I was able to reach out to a number of veterans in Dearborn Park (South Loop) where we lived to get them to join in. They were so grateful to be part of this event.

LARRY PIKE, US Army 1972-1974,1/44, 38th ADA Bde
I attended the 1986 Welcome Home Parade for Vietnam Veterans in Chicago. I was caught up in the last year of the Draft in 1972 and was prepared for any assignment that might come my way. After Basic Training at Ft. Polk, before going to AIT my class received Orders for

Korea. I was stationed at Reno Hill, Korea and quickly realized that the threat there was still very real. I was proud to have served as a Vietnam Era Veteran not knowing where I would be sent, but able to get the job done. I was also proud to have served with distinction with the many men and women, whom I still keep in contact with today. The Parade helped to connect the dots between service to country, honor, and comradeship.

JAMES FLYNN, 4th Infantry Division

Born and raised in Ireland in County Kerry as the son of dairy farmer, James came to Chicago at the age of 18 to visit his uncle. He met his wife Dorothy Moore from County Mayo, and we were married two years later. Around the same time, I got a letter from Uncle Sam telling me I was being drafted. I trained at Ft. Knox, KY and then was sent to Fort Polk, LA for advanced infantry training. Before that, I had two weeks furlough in Chicago. I used it to buy a trailer house and I took that and my wife to my Army Station. The first Sergeant was not happy with me and told me if the Army wanted me to have a wife, they would have issued me one. This unit was being trained specially for Vietnam.

I was the only one who brought my wife along, and after a few weeks, they said enough and sent me to Cook School. After graduating, I was sent to Fort Lewis, Washington to the 4th Infantry Division.

HAROLD WARP, 7/11th Arty ,25th Infantry Division, Vietnam (Pictures included, received from Howard J. McDonald, Ocean, N.J.) Harold, now deceased, was involved with VVA Chapter #242. Harold Warp owned his own Company and had been to our Reunions. His Father had started the Company which was FLEX-O-Glass, INC. started in 1924. He always published a story about Vietnam in his pamphlet that he sent out to all his customers every year. One of his latest ones was "Vietnam – Plus 50 Years." On Nov. 10th, 1968, after graduating from college Harold received his Draft Notice, and was to report for induction on December 10, 1968. After basic he went to Ft. Still, he learned to fire 105mm and 155mm Howitzers. He then went to Vietnam and arrived on May 29th, 1969. He was assigned to the 25th Infantry Division. He was assigned to Fire Support Base Pershing in the area between Saigon and Cambodia, just North of Trang Bang. His Team of six, with small flashlights in their mouths, cut charges, placed, and set fuses and fired 53 rounds in 12 minutes. They all received Bronze Stars with "V Device" for their counter-motor fire that night.

Later, Captain Zamory had an opening for Battery Clerk. Howard was offered the job and had to learn a whole new MOS. He got out of the Army as a SP5, doing morning reports, as well as orders, promotions, etc. He returned home from Vietnam on July 13th, 1970, with an Honorable Discharge."

Howard wrote the following: "So, if you see a veteran, especially a Vietnam Veteran, welcome him home, even if it is 50 years later. It still feels good to hear it. And thank them for their Service for putting their lives on the line. We honor our Patriots in doing so."

CHAPTER EIGHT

Agent Orange and the Other Toxic Agents

The environmental ghosts of Agent Orange, Blue, White, Green, Pink, and Purple, known as the rainbow herbicides, coupled with insecticide sprays and CS gas (a caustic powdered chemical) led to the decades long coverup by the Defense Department and Veterans Administration of the deadly effects of the toxicity of these substances.

From 1961 to 1971, approximately 20,000,000 (twenty million) gallons of Agent Orange and these other herbicides were aerial sprayed, power sprayed, individually hand sprayed and truck tanked sprayed in Vietnam, Thailand, Laos, Cambodia, Guam, America Samoa, and the Johnston Islands.

The Blue Water Navy also suffered from these actions. The air, water, cooking materials, drinking, and bathing water on land and at sea were affected as herbicides were deployed around the U.S. bases, ship, and personnel.

Agent Orange 2,4, -D=2,4,5 Trichlorophenoxyacetic Acid was invented by a German organization in the middle 1950's. They quickly realized the strength of the chemical which affected their employees and reduced their strength considerably. The U.S. chemical companies purchased U.S. rights to the original formula of the toxic agents. They then sold the agents to the U.S. government to be used in Asia.

ARPA (the Advanced Research Projects Agency) of the Defense Department which later morphed into DARPA (Defense Advanced Research Project Agency) was tasked with a carte blanche effort to introduce these toxic agents into Vietnam and elsewhere initially to produce an environmental and weather modification.

From 1958 forward ARPA led by William Godel and later Defense Department scientists, President Kennedy's advisors and the Ivy League intellectuals designated whiz kids led this effort to the detriment of veterans.

Starting in August 1963 the go ahead to introduce these toxins to Vietnam and other countries was supposed to be a "magic bullet" to greatly enhance defoliation.

This reality emanated from ARPA with reports from anthropologists and social scientists hired by consulting firms to provide their reports to the Defense Department. Subsequently, the coverup of the deadly effects of the toxicity continued for decades.

As noted, Vietnam veterans, their families, and children have suffered devastating losses since the end of the war in 1975.

Vets have been fighting for justice and benefits led by organizations like Vietnam Veterans of America and the veteran service officers of the other veteran organizations who serve as middlemen between the veterans and the VA to protect benefits due and provide appeals when benefits are denied.

The VA lists these causes of diseases "presumptives" (as used by the VA) which have been added over the course of the last four decades. There are 19 presumptives listed by the VA.

Veteran Service Officers have educated veterans with vital information based on the presumptives that have affected their current detrimental health conditions.

Congress passed the Agent Orange Act of 1991 stating that any veteran who served in Vietnam from 1962 to May 1975 was presumed to be exposed to Agent Orange and the other toxic herbicides.

In 2012, a $110 million campaign was initiated and paid for by the U.S. Government. It took five years to clean dioxin contaminated soil at Da Nang International Airport. Subsequently in 2018 the Vietnamese Government and the U.S. Government started the process of clearing up dioxin around the Bien Hoa Airport with a signed memorandum of intent. This rendition program initially started in 2000 and is a massive undertaking expected to cost $300 million at present.

One of the early heroes of the fight to achieve benefits for Agent Orange victims was Army Colonel Richard Christenson Jr., the first Director of the Army's "Agent Orange Task Force". He pursued military records and analyses that were key to the groundbreaking Agent Orange research conducted by Columbia Professors Jeanne M. Spellman and Steven D. Spellman.

Vietnam Veterans, their families and children are today still victims in the 21st century of the lack of transparency by the VA and the Defense Department....48 years after the end of the war.

Note: Sources used in compiling this information include the following 1. Silent Spring DEADLY AUTUMN for the Vietnam War by Patrick Hogan, Former Staff Sergeant, U.S. Army, Publisher: Whatnot Enterprises, LLC. Website: https://www.ssdavw.com. 2. The PENTAGON'S BRAIN, An Uncensored History of DARPA, America's Top Secret Miliary Research Agency by Annie Jacobsen, published by Back Bay Books, Little Brown, and Company.

THE AFTERMATH

In the aftermath of this seminal event, we are moving forward with all Vietnam Vets to demand changes of the Veterans Administration and define processes that result in acknowledging the effects of Agent Orange and other agents on Vietnam Veterans and their children.

Influenced by the music of the era this hope for change took the form of we will continue to assist our brother veterans and the veterans from other wars. We truly believe "you will never walk alone with hope in your heart." This event has propelled like gravitational waves in space a response of committing to push forward in the lives of these Vietnam Veterans and seize the opportunity to assist a newfound approach to guide this community.

The immediate outgrowth of the Parade that ultimately detached the previous false prognosis of the incapable Vietnam Veteran to one who had joined American society at all levels. All the American professions were represented as they marched in the Parade.

They were inspired by the visible impact the idea of a newfound brotherhood had on the temporary visitors who were amazed at the reception and welcome that the host city of Chicago offered to all veterans.

Flags are our memory of our history and projections into our future. The real power of Old Glory is the images of the struggles and doubts within the path followed by Veterans.

The American flag doesn't accept mistakes, it only shouts its truth.

Covid 19 and its mutations have left us with an abundance of fear. Entire cities were and continue to be faced with social distancing, lockdowns, closures, face masks, and constant handwashing. These were and are countermeasures. Yet, a lack of a vaccine until December 2020 for ages 16 and older caused many of our fellow vets coupled with their Agent Orange conditions to not survive the pandemic.

We will continue to march like the 176,000 Veterans at the Parade and instill a common goal for ourselves and the vets of other wars that follow us into posterity

PROLOGUE

Poem to honor Those Who Served: Diuturnity

Harold F. Beyne III

The timeless graying soldiers
emerging like stone sentinels
these Vietnam Veterans, enduring
many rites of passage, numbly
believing, when Johnny comes
Marching home again, hurrah, hurrah.

Scores of distant sounds,
magnetic, seizing, as a voice like
the sound of many waters;
pushing forward through rice paddies
with the Cobra gunships spitting
white hot rockets, thumping mini-guns
And grenades, echoing an ocean
beyond.

Mothers, sisters, wives, girlfriends,
And daughters; the women at
the barricades not wearing
sans-culottes like their sisters,
two centuries ago, but silently
embracing the flag of liberty
for their noble soldiers.

A return to sacrifices for
many doused in defoliants, wounded,
And maimed, striving to be successful
citizens of a true republic now
rendezvousing at a central city
that is embracing this mustering
as part of a deserved destiny.

64

The black granite wall presently
casts a shadow for many clicks
on a generation that asked
everything of a few in a different
war, now recalls these
shadowy warriors to a
place of honor.

1986

REFERENCES

"A Lam Tom's American Dream", by Connie Lauerman, Chicago Tribune, January 1, 1989

Chicago to Host Largest Vietnam Veterans Welcome Home Parade" by James Litke, June 7, 1986, Associated Press

Chicago Tribune, "At Peace at Last: After 11 Years and An Emotional Parade, Vietnam Vets Finally Feel Welcome" by William Mullen, June 10, 2011

Diuturnity

Litke, James, *Chicago's Welcome Home and Parade Launch and Organization*, Associated Press, June 7, 1986

Silent Spring DEADLY AUTUMN for the Vietnam War by Patrick Hogan, Former Staff Sergeant, U.S. Army, Publisher: Whatnot Enterprises, LLC. Website: https://www.ssdavw.com.

The PENTAGON'S BRAIN, An Uncensored History of DARPA, America's Top Secret Miliary Research Agency by Annie Jacobsen, published by Back Bay Books, Little Brown, and Company.

66

Appendix

Acknowledgement of Veterans

NAMES	UNIT
Adams, Tom R.	Riv. Div. 594
Ambrose, Fayard	4th Div.
Anderson, Dennis	USS Oriskeny Task Force 7
Andres, John	173rd Airborne
Anello, William	7th Bn. 11th Arty. 25th Inf Div
Arnswald, Thomas	USMCD81 Mortar
Beltner, Lance	1/7, 1st Cav
Beyne III, Harold F.	101st Abn. Div.
Boyd, Thomas	42EOD-1st Inf.Div.
Burch, Daniel	USS Navy B.T.
Cahill, James	178th Signal BN
Calkins, Kevin	1st Field Force 7 Bn. 13 Arty
Carr, Bill	9th Inf Div Medic
Clark, Pat	U.S. Navy
Clark, Steve	1st Cav
Clexton, Art	U.S.S. Clarke City
DeSalvo, Guy	USS Corrituck AV7 Navy
Dotson, James	D Co., 2/8| 1st Cav.
Duffy, Mike	Battery C, 7th Batallion, 9th Arty
Edgar, Bruce	3rd Marine Div
Edwards, John	91 APS – Airforce/Navy
Flynn, James	704 Maint. BN 4th Inf. Div
Fuggiti, Robert J	1st Cav
Garcia, Benito, R	173rd 65-66, 716 M.P. Btln, 1966, 101st Abn Div. 66-67, 82nd Abn 3rd Brigade 67-68
Gelburd, Michael	17th Cav – American
Ginnelly, Tom	1st BN 32nd Inf. 7th Inf. Div
George, Janis	AVVA
Geranry, John	USS Aircraft Carrier
Grandberg, Mike	3rd Recon
Granbey, Mike	3rd Mar. Recon BN
Hayes, Pat	U.S. Army
Henk, Jim	C/2/502nd 101st Abn Div
Hennes, Leo	537th PSC Bien Hoa
Heim, George	2/17 Arty
Heinrich, John	48th Assault Helicopter Da Nang

Huffman, Don	11th Brigade Americal
Iacullo, Ken	2/502/101st
Jennings, Jim	1/7th Cav 1st Cav 66-67
Johnsen, Dennis	30th MSS
Kariewiec, Steven	Bravo 4/3, 11th Inf
Klinger, Edward P.	10th FCS
Klusman, John	173rd Abn
Korovesis, Steve	3rd/187th
Kukurba, Peter	3rd Force Recon
Lancaster, James	LST 838
Layden, Mike	1st Marine Air Wing
Lieggi, Lorenzo	457th Signal BN
Lisitza, Bruce	118th M.P. Airborne
Lockhart, Charles	SSBN Blue Nuclear Sub
Lowery. Bob	Big Red One
Lymperopulos, Mark	7th Eng. BN 1st Marine Div
Lynch, Allen CMOH	1/12 1st Cav
Mangas, Dan	5th Special Forces (ABN)
Manna, John	2nd Ranger BN 2nd Inv. Div
Manna, Ross	1st Log Phu Bai
Mayer, Jim	85th Mtce. Co
McGill, Roger	¾ Cavalry – 25th Inf Division
McKenna, Dennis	1st Mobile Communications
McAllum, Barry	U.S. Army Korea 1/23rd Inf.
McEnaney, Jim H.	3/4 Cav, 25 Inf Div
Meril, Jim	1st Armor
Mindak, Jim	USAF 12th C.E.S.
Morrison, Kevin P.	NSF HOA USN
Morrison, Roger	9th Inf. Div. 11th Armor Cav
Mulcrone, Brian J.	23 Inf Div Americal
Nilsson, Dennis	65th Combat Eng. 25th Inf.
O'Brian, Pat	U.S. Army – 1st Log.
O'Brian, Rich	DCo. 2/8th 1st Cav
O'Donnell, Chris	VMA 543
O'Grady, Donnie	U.S. Army
O'Leary, Bob	4th BN, 11th Marines Lima Battery
Oller, Ed	11th MACV Team 6 1st Mar. Div. Corpsman
Olsen, Steve	101st ABN Div – door gunner
Passarella, Marty	34th Armor – 25th Inf. Div.
Pearson, George	1st/22nd – 4th Inf. Div
Pellicano, Richard	3rd Support Brigade Europe
Piattoni, Russ	USS Sacramento

Pietrosiewicz, Rich	3 Bn Marines
Pike, Lawrerance	38th ADA Brigade 1/44
Ponoeses, Chris	Echo Co 2/26 7 Marines
Poplawski, Jerry	USS Enterprise VF 96
Redwine, James	9th Inf. Div
Reilly, Mick	1st Brigade, 5th Inf.
Reid, John	2/14th – 25th Inf Div
Roess, Roger	116 M.P. Bn.
Rolan, Jorge Rafael	Sgt. Co. A 121st Sig BN& Calvary Scout
Runtz, John	MACV
Runtz, Bob	11th Cav Support
Ryan, Jim	9th Inf. Division
Sachs, Richard	LRP. 101 Abn. Div/75th Rangers
Saladino, Carlos	173rd Airborne & 25th Inf Div
Sangari, Sargis	2nd ID, 25th – SOCOM 96th
Schaefer, Allan	Army 71st Arty
Simons, Frederik S.	SOG Helicopter Pilot
Smith, R Dennis	618 Tac Control Squadron
Stephan, Peter	187th Med BN
Sulimowski, Dominic	534th M.P.
Sunwing T. Leung	Msgt U.S. Air Force
Taft, Adam	Corpsman, U.S. Navy
Talley, James E	7th Fleet M.P. Japan
Thalmann, Scott	1st. Mar. Div
Tom, Lam	South Vietnam Assoc.
Toscano, Mickey	U.S. Marines
Valentine, Ron	7th Comm. Bn, 1st Mar. Div 67-68, 69-70
Walczak, Ron	23rd. MP/CO Americal
Warp, Harold	Artillery, 25th Inf. Div.
Weber, Donald	2/9 Marines
Weber, Steven	432 Recon Wing
Weber, Marvin	5th Special Forces Group
Welther, J. Doc	3rd Mar Div 2/4
Wiemhoff, John	1st CAV
Zamorski,, Nancy	Ft. Bragg, XVIII Airborne

The following five Vietnam Veterans died of Covid 19 between February 2020 and May 2021. These five former servicemen also had underlying agent orange issues.

Don Freeman	U.S. Army
Bob Brieske	1st Marine Division
Mike Mika	U.S. Army
Walter J. Blasé	M.P. U.S. Army
Larry Bohl	U.S. Army

ABOUT THE AUTHORS

Roger McGill and Harold F. Beyne (Harry), first met during the planning phases of the 1986 Parade. Roger headed up the planning committee and Harry served on the committee in a number of capacities.

Through the years their friendship has grown with Roger providing invaluable advice to Harry and a number of his friends and relatives regarding VA benefit programs and services. During the past 10 years, Harry became quite involved with Vietnam Veterans of America (VVA) Chapter 242, with Roger and had been involved since

1985. Roger, Carlos Saladino, and Marty Pasarella. initiated this small gathering back in 2015. Today, they meet every Tuesday first at the Dunkin' Donuts in Niles, IL., which is so generously provided by  the owner and generally reconvene in small groups at Kappy's American Grill, Morton Grove where they are always warmly greeted by its manager George Alpogianis. The group pays tribute to all Veterans on Memorial Day, Vietnam Veterans Day, and Veterans Day attending and participating in ceremonies in the Chicagoland area. Pictured at one such event are Harry (Left) and Roger.

Their friendship as well as the lasting bond formed among the many members of 242, many of whom are listed in this section, have served to support the medical and overall health, including PTSD, needs of these veterans. This book is a tribute to them.

Harry Beyne served in the U.S. Army from March 13, 1968, until December 21, 1970, when he received an early out and honorable discharge to attend college. Basic and AIT training took place at Ft. Leonard Wood, MO. Then onto Ft. Benjamin Harrison, Indianapolis, IN for more training. In August 1968 Harry transferred to Ft. Dix New Jersey for nine months with orders coming in April 1969 for Vietnam. Vietnam service with 101st Airborne Division where he was stationed at Bien Hoa and then later transferred to Phu Bai, where he remained until leaving Vietnam.

Harry obtained his bachelors from the University of Illinois, Chicago, and his master's in public administration from Roosevelt University. Through the years he was involved in a number of entrepreneurial ventures primarily focused on real estate valuation and appraisal and then real estate development and construction.

Harry and his wife Sarah reside in Northbrook, Illinois. They have a son Christopher, daughter-in-law Casey, grandson Carter James and daughter Helen. They are richly blessed to have such a wonderful family.

Roger McGill was drafted into the U.S. Army on June 3, 1964. He attended Basic Training at Ft. Knox, KY., and after Basic went to AIT at Ft. Knox, and was trained as a Cavalry Scout 11D10. He then went after AIT to Ft. Hood, TX. A Troop 2/1st Cavalry, 2nd Armor Division "Hell on Wheels". Shortly thereafter, he came down on orders to go to the 3Rd Squadron, 4th Cavalry – Schofield Barracks, Hawaii, was assigned there to HQ & HQ Troop in the S-1 Section and was the RTO/Driver for the Executive Officer of the Squadron, and held that position, and did the same when they came down on orders to go to Vietnam, Cu Chi, with the 25th Infantry Division – all this taking place in 1965 – 1966.

Roger was Drafted while he was working for the Telephone Co. where he started in 1963, and when he came back from Vietnam, he went back to work for the Telephone Co. and worked as an Installer, Repairman, Tester, in Superior District. He then worked in the Special Service Center taking care of Chicago's Larger organizations and from there went to Planning and Engineering at Headquarters 225 W. Randolph. and then to Lake View/Edgewater/Rogers Park on the North side of the City of Chicago. After 30 years of services, he retired.

In 1985 I went to the WALL in Washington, D. C. as there were 22 Vietnam Veterans that I served with that were KIA in Vietnam in the years I was there. When I was there, I met other Vietnam Veterans and they told me about a Vietnam Veterans WELCOME HOME Parade that was going to happen in NYC on May 5th, 1985, and they said if you go, we will also go, and I did. Both being at the WALL in D.C. and then the NYC Parade was very moving for me. When I came home, I got involved here in Chicago and became the Program Chairman for the Chicago Vietnam Veterans Parade and ran that committee.

Roger then went to work for Vietnam Veterans of America Veterans Service Office (VSO) down at the VA Regional Office on Taylor Street. He has been there for over 12 years now helping Veterans with claims. He also belongs to VVA Chapter #242 Chicago since 1985. Roger was the Co-Chairman for the Chicago Vietnam Veterans Memorial at the Chicago River Walk and was on the committee for the Illinois Vietnam Veterans Memorial in Springfield, IL. at Oak Ridge Cemetery

Roger is married to Cathy Deignan/McGill for 53 years and they have three adult children and two Grandchildren. John & Carrie Karsakow/McGill – and son Charlie McGill, Daughter – Colette McGill, and James & Trish O'Connor/McGill and daughter Ailish McGill. He and his wife share their gratitude for the blessings of having such a wonderful family.